Mary Misunderstood

A Closer Look at the Marys in the Bible

Pamela Rose Williams

Christianity Every Day

Albuquerque, NM

Mary Misunderstood: A Closer Look at the Marys in the Bible

Pamela Rose Williams

A Christianity Every Day™ Resource

Copyright © 2017 by Christianity Every Day

Published by Christianity Every Day, United States of America
www.christianityeveryday.com

Library of Congress Data

Williams, Pamela Rose, 1960-
        Mary Misunderstood: A Closer Look at the Marys in the Bible

        ISBN: 978-0-9996173-0-4
        Library of Congress Control Number: 2017917420

Scripture quotations are from the Holy Bible, King James Version. Printed in the United States of America.

Table of Contents

Acknowledgements

This little book is a work that has been many years in the making. It is the project that was always set aside because other duties called. I am thankful to the Lord for maintaining my vision on this work and nudging me to get it finished. Throughout the years when someone would mention a Mary from the Bible and especially when I knew from my study that what they were saying was not true, His still small voice would remind me to finish this task. Thank you Lord also for the talent and abilities that you have given to me to write down what I have learned so that I could share it with others.

I am forever grateful to my husband for sticking by my side throughout what seemed to be hundreds of edits. He gave great suggestions and helped me to better clarify my thoughts and words on the pages from the "reader's" perspective. He is a wonderful and brave man—he endured the grueling process of editing the editor! In addition, I am blessed that he is an excellent writer and a Bible teacher which only made my study of the Marys more precise and complete. Thank you honey for helping me to press on.

I am thankful to my daughter Candi and her husband Eric and EA Studios Photography for providing the lovely roses photograph for the front cover. And once again, thank you to Michael for helping to complete the cover design. Great job!

Finally, I am thankful to you, my reader, for having the open mind to consider what I am sharing about the Marys in the Bible. I have dealt with some sensitive issues on these pages. I encourage you to study your Bible and let the Scriptures speak the truth to you.

Preface

Several years ago, I was preparing a devotional lesson for our Ladies' Tea and I wanted to present the account of how Mary anointed Jesus with oil as a sign of her love for the Master. While I was preparing, I read something that made me question whether or not I was presenting the correct Mary. This caused me to study deeper because I suddenly realized that the name "Mary" is a very popular name in the New Testament. In fact, throughout the New Testament we may find the name "Mary" fifty-one times.

During my study, I was reminded of how very important it is to allow Scripture to prove Scripture, rather than to trust in something that I had thought I learned many years ago. The Holy Spirit reminded me that *"All scripture is given by inspiration of God, and is profitable for doctrine, for reproof, for correction, for instruction in righteousness: That the man of God may be perfect, throughly furnished unto all good works."* (2 Timothy 3:16, 17)

As you read on, I pray that you will use the Bible to look up passages and to compare them one to another. If your Bible is not handy right now, go get it before you continue this journey. I encourage you to read the passages in context and use the whole Word of God to sort it out. In doing so, I know that you too will find that "Mary" in the Bible can be so easily misunderstood as you realize that there are at least six different people with that name!

Chapter 1 Mary Magdalene

Mary Magdalene is one of the most famous Marys in the Bible, second only to Mary, the mother of Jesus. Throughout history she has been portrayed as a prostitute, a woman delivered from demonic possession and even the wife of Christ and mother of His children. The confusion over who Mary really was stems from teachings based on tradition instead of the truth of the Bible.

MODERN BELIEFS AND HISTORICAL CULT FOLLOWING

The release of the movie Da Vinci Code in 2006 has reinforced erroneous opinions of Mary Magdalene that have existed for centuries. The movie is based upon the novel of the same name, which has been considered one of the best-selling English novels of the 21st century. The movie was highly protested by Bible believers and embraced by others as it portrayed Mary of Magdalene as the wife of Jesus (1).

It is commonly believed that Mary Magdalene is "the woman who was a sinner," as found in Luke 7:37-38 or that she was unchaste. Some even say she was a prostitute, but the Bible does not support this. This idea was first introduced in 591 A.D., when Pope Gregory the Great gave an Easter sermon in which he erroneously declared that the "prostitute" of Luke 7:37 was Mary Magdalene of Luke 8 (2). The passage in question was not speaking of Mary Magdalene, instead it is speaking of another Mary. More on this later.

It is unclear why Pope Gregory portrayed Mary Magdalene in this way but his words gave birth to the idea that Mary Magdalene was something that cannot be supported by Scripture. Thankfully, in 1969, The Second Vatican Council corrected centuries of misunderstanding by acknowledging that there was no basis for her identification as a prostitute (3). Sadly, since this misinformation was repeated over and over again for so many years, even today most people still believe she was a prostitute.

ANCIENT ROOTS AND EARLY MINISTRY

Mary's hometown in Biblical times, Magdala (Magadan, Dalmanutha), was on the northwest shore of the Sea of Galilee. It was known as an area that was fertile and great for fishing. Today an Arabic village is located just west of the ancient site and is called Migdal (al-Mijdal or "the tower" in Arabic). In Greek this place was called "Taricheae" which was named for a popular type of pickled fish that was produced there (4)(5). For this reason, Mary is called Mary Magdalene because it was often customary in Biblical times to be named for the town in which you were born.

Jesus met Mary Magdalene early in His ministry while He was preaching in Magdala and the surrounding areas of Galilee. According to Luke 8:1-2, Jesus cast seven demons out of Mary. Gratitude to her great Deliverer prompted her to become His follower even though there were few others following at this time. Therefore, we see Mary Magdalene was one of the women who accompanied Jesus throughout his journeys concluding with his final journey to Jerusalem (Matthew 27:55-56; Mark 15:40-41; Luke 23:55-56).

Mary Magdalene is listed as one of the Marys at the foot of the cross when Jesus was crucified. She stood near the cross where she remained until all was over, and the body was taken down and laid in Joseph's tomb.

John 19:25 Now there stood by the cross of Jesus his mother, and his mother's sister, Mary the wife of Cleophas, and ***Mary Magdalene.***

Mark 15:40–41 There were also women looking on afar off: among whom was ***Mary Magdalene***, and Mary the mother of James the less and of Joses, and Salome; 41 (Who also, when he was in Galilee, followed him, and ministered unto him;) and many other women which came up with him unto Jerusalem.

Likewise, the Bible tells us that Mary Magdalene was the first to see the Lord after His resurrection and also the one who announced Jesus' resurrection to the others.

Mark 16:9–11 Now when Jesus was risen early the first day of the week, he appeared ***first to Mary Magdalene***, out of whom he had cast seven devils. 10 And she went and told them that had been with him, as they mourned and wept. 11 And they, when they had heard that he was alive, and had been seen of her, believed not.

Meeting Jesus profoundly changed the life of Mary Magdalene. When He arose from the dead, victorious, she could not wait to tell everyone about the most exciting thing that had ever happened to her.

CHARACTER TRAIT FOR MARY MAGDALENE - COMMITTED

Mary Magdalene was a committed follower of Jesus. Her life, after meeting Jesus, reflected one of unwavering gratitude and servant-hood for the Master who saved her from the demons that used to control her life. She was devoted to Him, as was her reasonable service to Him for freeing her (Romans 12:1). Her commitment serves as an example of a changed life.

When I think of Mary Magdalene I think of how very committed she was to Jesus after He rescued her from those demons. If you think about it, all of us should be committed to Jesus because He saved us and changed our lives. Here are some great Bible Verses to meditate upon when you think of this Mary:

Mark 8:34–35 And when he had called the people unto him with his disciples also, he said unto them, Whosoever will come after me, let him deny himself, and take up his cross, and follow me. 35 For whosoever will save his life shall lose it; but whosoever shall lose his life for my sake and the gospel's, the same shall save it.

Mark 15:40–41 There were also women looking on afar off: among whom was Mary Magdalene, and Mary the mother of James the less and of Joses, and Salome; 41 (Who also, when he was in Galilee, followed him, and ministered unto him;) and many other women which came up with him unto Jerusalem.

Luke 23:49 And all his acquaintance, and the women that followed him from Galilee, stood afar off, beholding these things.

John 19:25 Now there stood by the cross of Jesus his mother, and his mother's sister, Mary the wife of Cleophas, and Mary Magdalene.

THINGS TO THINK ABOUT AND DO
1. Think about a time when you had wrong information about someone. What did you do with that information? If you think you handled that situation improperly, what could you have done differently?

2. Spreading information about someone is often times called gossip. Find three verses in the Bible that caution against gossip (also look for keywords like backbiting and talebearer)

Chapter 2 The Other Mary

As we continue on in the Bible we see another Mary who has no other real distinguishing factor, nor any real memorable account. She is sometimes mistaken as Mary of Nazareth, the mother of Jesus, mostly because she has two sons with the same names of James and Joses. Let's take a look and see how we can distinguish The Other Mary from Mary of Nazareth.

JUST AN OTHER MARY

We learn in Matthew 27:56 that her sons James and Joses are different from the James and Joses mentioned as Jesus' brothers in Matthew 13:55 and Mark 6:3. In fact, there are several different individuals named James in the New Testament:

James, the son of Zebedee and Salome and the brother of the Apostle John, also one of the twelve apostles (Matthew 4:12, Mark 1:19, Mark 17:11, Luke 5:10). Also known as James the elder.

James, the son of Alphaeus or Cleophas, (Mary's husband). This James is also called "James the Less" and "James the Younger" (Mark 15:40) and the brother of Joses. (Matthew 27:56). This title "Less" most likely is used because he was younger than James of Zebedee. James was a cousin to Jesus (since Mary was the sister of Jesus' mother [John 19:25]).

James, the brother of Jesus and son of Mary of Nazareth (Matthew 13:55; Mark 6:3; Luke 6:16; Galatians 1:19).

Not too hard to get confused here … there are almost as many James and Joses as there are Marys in the Bible! However, this Mary, whom we simply call "The Other Mary" is again seen as the mother of James and Joses found in the following verses:

Matthew 27:55–56 And many women were there beholding afar off, which followed Jesus from Galilee, ministering unto him: 56 Among which was Mary Magdalene, and Mary the mother of James and Joses, and the mother of Zebedee's children.

This Mary also appears in several areas of Scripture and it is easy to get confused unless you compare the Scriptures side by side. In the Bible we can see that:

She was the sister of Mary of Nazareth, Jesus' mother, and one of three Marys at the foot of the cross:

John 19:25 Now there **stood by the cross of Jesus** his mother, and **his mother's sister, Mary the wife of Cleophas**, and Mary Magdalene.

She went with Mary Magdalene to anoint the body of Jesus at His tomb (sepulchre):

Matthew 27:61 And there was Mary Magdalene, and **the other Mary**, sitting over against the sepulchre.

Matthew 28:1 In the end of the sabbath, as it began to dawn toward the first day of the week, came Mary Magdalene and **the other Mary** to see the sepulchre.

Mark 16:1 And when the sabbath was past, Mary Magdalene, and *Mary the mother of James*, and Salome, had bought sweet spices, that they might come and anoint him.

HARMONY OF THE GOSPELS

When comparing any character or event in Scripture, a valuable reference that could be found from many sources is called the Harmony of the Gospels. A great example of this is shown in the following listing of "The Other Mary" at the foot of the cross in all of the Gospels:

The Other Mary At the Foot of the Cross			
Matthew	**Mark**	**Luke**	**John**
(Matthew 27:55-56) And many women were there beholding afar off, which followed Jesus from Galilee, ministering unto him: 56 Among which was Mary Magdalene, and Mary the mother of James and Joses, and the mother of Zebedee:s children.	(Mark 15:40-41) There were also women looking afar off: among whom was Mary Magdalene, and Mary the mother of James the less and of Joses, and Salome; 41 (Who also when he was in Galilee, followed him, and ministered unto him;) and many other women which came up with him unto Jerusalem.	(Luke 23:49) And all his acquaintance, and the women that followed him from Galilee, stood afar off, beholding these things.	(John 19:25) Now there stood by the cross of Jesus his mother, and his mother's sister, Mary the wife of Cleophas, and Mary Magdalene.

CHARACTER TRAIT FOR THE OTHER MARY - FAITHFUL/LOYAL

Although The Other Mary had a family relationship with Jesus, she also demonstrated that she was faithful in the way she loyally supported Him and His mother. For example, The Other Mary was near to Jesus at the cross and at the resurrection. Though she did not play a large role when compared to the rest of the crowd, her personal presence in these last hours was invaluable to Jesus and His mother. The Other Mary showed that some people in your crowd of friends may not necessarily do a lot of things other than just be there for you in your time of need.

Some Bible verses that come to mind for the faithfulness and loyalty demonstrated by The Other Mary are:

Psalm 31:23 O love the LORD, all ye his saints: For the LORD preserveth the faithful, And plentifully rewardeth the proud doer.

Matthew 25:21 His lord said unto him, Well done, thou good and faithful servant: thou hast been faithful over a few things, I will make thee ruler over many things: enter thou into the joy of thy lord.

Matthew 26:35 Peter said unto him, Though I should die with thee, yet will I not deny thee. Likewise also said all the disciples.

Luke 16:10 He that is faithful in that which is least is faithful also in much: and he that is unjust in the least is unjust also in much.

THINGS TO THINK ABOUT AND DO

1. Consider a time when you stood by a friend through thick and thin. How do you suppose your friend felt about that? Now think of someone who needs a loyal friend. What can you do to show some loyalty to that person in need?

2. Friends are priceless and friendships are like gardens, they need to be cultivated. List three things that can be done to cultivate friendships.

Chapter 3 Mary of Bethany

Mary of Bethany, like the other Marys in the Bible is not always remembered for whom she really was. She had a famous brother named Lazarus, whom Jesus raised from death. She also had a sister named Martha whom, like many sisters, was different from Mary in how she did things. Her relationship with her sister reveals to us that our approach to how we do things is very important.

ARE YOU A MARTHA OR A MARY?

People who are familiar with Martha and Mary know that they are sisters. While Jesus was joining them for supper, Martha was the one who was busy in the kitchen working. Meanwhile, her sister Mary was at the feet of Jesus listening to everything He had to say. In Christian circles sometimes we are called a Martha or a Mary.

Calling ourselves a "Martha" is what we say when we are caught up in the doing of something and forget to take time to just be with the people we love. Of course, calling ourselves a "Mary" is what we say when we are the one socializing in the midst of the people we love instead of in the background preparing. Both of these roles are important. However, take a look at Luke 10:39-42 where the Lord reminded Martha that Mary's devotion to Him was a "good part":

Luke 10:39–42 And she had a sister called Mary, which also sat at Jesus' feet, and heard his word. 40 But Martha was cumbered about much serving, and came to him, and said, Lord, dost thou not care that my sister hath left me to serve alone? bid her therefore that she help me. 41 And Jesus answered and said unto her, Martha, Martha, thou art careful and troubled about many things: 42 But one thing is needful: and Mary hath chosen that good part, which shall not be taken away from her.

HISTORICAL ROOTS AND MISUNDERSTANDINGS

The name Bethany in Biblical times is interpreted as a house or place of unripe figs. It is located just east on the outskirts of Jerusalem, near the Mount of Olives, about 1 1/2 miles from Jerusalem. This is the place where Jesus was when He ascended to Heaven (Luke 24:50). Today it is called Azariyeh or Lazariyeh ("the place of Lazarus")(7). Let's compare two accounts from Matthew and Luke in the following table which involves another time when Mary of Bethany was at the feet of Jesus.

Mary of Bethany at Jesus' Feet	
(Matthew 26:6-13) Now when Jesus was in Bethany, in the house of Simon the leper, 7 There came unto him a woman having an alabaster box of very precious ointment, and poured it on his head, as he sat at meat. 8 But when his disciples saw it, they had indignation, saying, To what purpose is this waste? 9 For this ointment might have been sold for much, and given to the poor. 10 When Jesus understood it, he said unto them, Why trouble ye the woman? For she hath wrought a good work upon me. 11 For ye have the poor always with you; but me ye have not always. 12 For in that she has poured this ointment on my body, she did it for my burial. 13 Verily I say unto you, Wheresoever this gospel shall be preached in the whole world, there shall also this, that this woman hath done, be told for a memorial to her.	(Luke 7:37-39) And, behold, a woman in the city, which was a sinner, when she knew that Jesus sat at meat at the Pharisee's house, brought an alabaster box of ointment, 38 And stood at his feet behind him weeping, and began to wash his feet with her tears and id wipe them with the hairs of her head, and kissed his feet, and anointed them with the ointment. 39 Now when the Pharisee which had bidden him saw it, he spake within himself, saying, This man, if he were a prophet, would have known who and what manner of woman this is that toucheth him: for she is a sinner.

When looking at these two passages we must ask ourselves "Why was Mary pouring this precious perfume upon Jesus?" Some say that because Lazarus, Martha, and Mary were close friends of Jesus, they had anointing spices from wise men for Jesus' final anointing and body preparation. They also claim that these were the spices that were given by the wise men at Jesus' birth. It is very possible that Jesus' mother gave those spices to Him to be used at the appropriate time.

Regardless of the origin of the spices, Mary was performing an act of extreme humility, devotion and selfless love. And Jesus made it clear that His anointing was more important than giving that money to the poor.

> John 12:1–8 Then Jesus six days before the passover came to Bethany, where Lazarus was which had been dead, whom he raised from the dead. 2 There they made him a supper; and Martha served: but Lazarus was one of them that sat at the table with him. 3 Then took Mary a pound of ointment of spikenard, very costly, and anointed the feet of Jesus, and wiped his feet with her hair: and the house was filled with the odour of the ointment. 4 Then saith one of his disciples, Judas Iscariot, Simon's son, which should betray him, 5 Why was not this ointment sold for three hundred pence, and given to the poor? 6 This he said, not that he cared for the poor; but because he was a thief, and had the bag, and bare what was put therein. 7 Then said Jesus, Let her alone: against the day of my burying hath she kept this. 8 For the poor always ye have with you; but me ye have not always.

If we look a little closer into this anointing by Mary what do we see? It says: "Then Jesus six days before the passover came to Bethany..." We see that this was the last Passover that Jesus would celebrate because the time of His death was drawing near (John 12:23-25). Therefore, this anointing had a special significance. But, Judas was not happy that Mary used this expensive ointment to anoint the feet of Jesus. In response, Jesus said in John 12:7-8 for him to leave her alone.

Why would our Saviour say this to Judas? Jesus knew what was in Judas' heart. In fact, Judas was a thief (John 12:6) and a devil (John 6:70). Judas just wanted the perfume so he could sell it and steal the money. Jesus alluded to the fact that He was leaving the earth soon and what she was doing was more important. He added that we would always have opportunity to give to the poor and needy. Mary's act was for the here and now. Jesus was here and now. Jesus is here and now. What are you doing to show your love for the Master?

One last observation. Do you see it in Luke 7:37-39 in the chart previously? Mary of Bethany was "the woman in the city which was a sinner." She was not Mary Magdalene as has been mistaken and repeated since A. D. 591! This is why it is so important to let Scripture prove Scripture (Study to show thyself approved unto God, a workman that needeth not to be ashamed, rightly dividing the word of truth. 2 Timothy 2:15).

Notice, 2 Timothy 2:15 does not say that we should trust someone else to do our studying for us; it says "Study to show thyself approved". My husband often says, "If you know the normal, the abnormal will stand out." This is so true! If you know what the Bible says, when you hear things that are not supported by the Bible, the Holy Spirit will bring Scripture to mind which confirms what is true. This is why we must "rightly divide the word of truth". The only way we are able to do this is to spend time in the Word. Have you been looking up these Scriptures that I am pointing out?

CHARACTER TRAIT FOR MARY OF BETHANY - SELFLESS LOVE

Mary of Bethany had a great love for Jesus because she knew she was a sinner and He was her Saviour. She demonstrated a selfless love for Him because He demonstrated a selfless love for her (1 John 4:19). Her selflessness was motivated by love, not obligation. This is why

Jesus said "Mary hath chosen that good part, which shall not be taken away from her" (Luke 10:42). Acts of service motivated by a love of God and love of our neighbor will always be remembered by God (1 Corinthians 3:9-15).

Here are some Bible verses that make me think of Mary of Bethany:

Ephesians 4:29 Let no corrupt communication proceed out of your mouth, but that which is good to the use of edifying, that it may minister grace unto the hearers.

Philippians 2:3–4 Let nothing be done through strife or vainglory; but in lowliness of mind let each esteem other better than themselves. 4 Look not every man on his own things, but every man also on the things of others.

1 Timothy 6:17–19 Charge them that are rich in this world, that they be not highminded, nor trust in uncertain riches, but in the living God, who giveth us richly all things to enjoy; 18 That they do good, that they be rich in good works, ready to distribute, willing to communicate; 19 Laying up in store for themselves a good foundation against the time to come, that they may lay hold on eternal life.

THINGS TO THINK ABOUT AND DO

1. What is the object of your devotion? Better yet, who is the object of your devotion? Devotion requires selfless acts of love. Think of one thing you can do for someone today that will prove your selflessness.

2. Look in your Bible and list at least three other people whom were selfless.

Chapter 4 Mary, the Mother of John Mark

The next Mary that we see in the Bible is not one that is spoken much of today. She is Mary, the mother of John Mark. She is mentioned only once in the New Testament. Her contribution is great and I think you will enjoy reading a little about her.

Mary was the mother of John Mark, the author of the Gospel according to Mark. Let's look at this Mary a little closer. Here is what I found about her:

Her home was used as a gathering place for prayer meetings (Acts 12:12).

After Peter was freed from prison by an angel, he fled to Mary's house to hide (Acts 12:11-17).

She had a brother named Barnabas, whom was the uncle to her son, John Mark (Marcus) (Colossians 4:10)

POOR RHODA

When Peter went to Mary's house in Acts 12:11-17, there were a number of the Jerusalem brethren gathered together for a prayer vigil on Peter's behalf. There is no mention of Mary having a husband but she did have a young maid named Rhoda. You must read this account to appreciate poor Rhoda, how excited she was to see Peter – and the others who thought she was insane.

To set the context: Peter was awaiting trial at Jerusalem where he was imprisoned by Herod Agrippa just prior to the Passover. For several days the Church had engaged in fervent prayer for his release

(Acts 12:5). When Peter escaped from prison (Acts 12:14) he went directly to Mary's house where his friends were praying. He wanted to let them know that he had been released and to go tell James (the brother of Jesus) and others. Look at how the Bible records this account:

> Acts 12:6–17 And when Herod would have brought him forth, the same night Peter was sleeping between two soldiers, bound with two chains: and the keepers before the door kept the prison. 7 And, behold, the angel of the Lord came upon him, and a light shined in the prison: and he smote Peter on the side, and raised him up, saying, Arise up quickly. And his chains fell off from his hands. 8 And the angel said unto him, Gird thyself, and bind on thy sandals. And so he did. And he saith unto him, Cast thy garment about thee, and follow me. 9 And he went out, and followed him; and wist not that it was true which was done by the angel; but thought he saw a vision. 10 When they were past the first and the second ward, they came unto the iron gate that leadeth unto the city; which opened to them of his own accord: and they went out, and passed on through one street; and forthwith the angel departed from him. 11 And when Peter was come to himself, he said, Now I know of a surety, that the Lord hath sent his angel, and hath delivered me out of the hand of Herod, and from all the expectation of the people of the Jews. 12 And when he had considered the thing, he came to the house of Mary the mother of John, whose surname was Mark; where many were gathered together praying. 13 And as Peter knocked at the door of the gate, a damsel came to hearken, named Rhoda. 14 And when she knew Peter's voice, she opened not the gate for gladness, but ran in, and told how Peter stood before the gate. 15 And they said unto her, Thou art mad. But she constantly affirmed that it was even so. Then said they, It is his angel. 16 But Peter

continued knocking: and when they had opened the door, and saw him, they were astonished. 17 But he, beckoning unto them with the hand to hold their peace, declared unto them how the Lord had brought him out of the prison. And he said, Go shew these things unto James, and to the brethren. And he departed, and went into another place.

Isn't that wild?! There they were, praying for Peter's release and then he appeared at the door. No wonder they thought Rhoda had lost her mind! They were so busy praying for Peter's release that they could not understand what she was saying … that Peter was there! This was the work of God and truly a miracle. I call it a "faith builder" … if there was anyone doubting the release of Peter before he popped in for a visit; certainly now they believed! Sometimes we get too caught up in the religious "stuff" that we miss seeing God at work. Don't you agree?

On a side note—Mary's house, a meeting place for Jesus' followers, which was inside the city walls of Jerusalem is interesting to consider. It seems to have had a courtyard sort of entry which gave the main entry privacy from the street. It also had a large gathering room (8). Some believe that this was the same house that had an upper chamber where the Apostles met on the day of Pentecost as seen in Acts 2, however I have not found evidence of this in the Bible.

How great is it to read about these special women of God? This Mary's house was the meeting place and she was not concerned about having a house full – continually. She had the means, the desire and the selflessness to make things happen. Mary the Mother of John Mark had a special gift of hospitality and she was faithful in giving to her brothers and sisters in Christ.

CHARACTER TRAIT FOR MARY THE MOTHER OF JOHN MARK - GENEROSITY AND HOSPITALITY

Generosity and hospitality sometimes do not come easily. God is a loving and giving God and when we seek a close relationship with Him we are inspired to be generous and hospitable. Mary the Mother of John Mark generously gave of her finances and home to physically provide for the Church. Her act of hospitality provided healing for the emotional and spiritual needs of those concerned about Peter's imprisonment.

Take a look at these Bible verses that remind me of Mary the Mother of John Mark:

Matthew 6:21 For where your treasure is, there will your heart be also.

Matthew 10:42 And whosoever shall give to drink unto one of these little ones a cup of cold water only in the name of a disciple, verily I say unto you, he shall in no wise lose his reward.

Luke 12:33 Sell that ye have, and give alms; provide yourselves bags which wax not old, a treasure in the heavens that faileth not, where no thief approacheth, neither moth corrupteth.

Romans 12:13 Distributing to the necessity of saints; given to hospitality.

2 Corinthians 9:7 Every man according as he purposeth in his heart, so let him give; not grudgingly, or of necessity: for God loveth a cheerful giver.

1 Peter 4:8–10 And above all things have fervent charity among yourselves: for charity shall cover the multitude of sins. 9 Use hospitality one to another without grudging. 10 As every man hath received the gift, even so minister the same one to another, as good stewards of the manifold grace of God.

THINGS TO THINK ABOUT AND DO

1. Give some thought to how you can be this Mary today. Do you have something that you can give to your brothers and sisters to help them to grow closer to Christ? Can you open your home? Maybe not for a weekly meeting forever, but consider a weekly Bible study for a few weeks.

2. Consider opening your home to some brothers and sisters visiting from out of town. I know that we have been blessed many times by people who were not afraid to open their homes to us when we were visiting from afar. You can be a blessing just as Mary the mother of John Mark was because giving can be more than just putting money into an offering plate.

Chapter 5 Mary the Labourer

This next Mary is perhaps the least known of anyone. She was mentioned by Paul when he wrote a letter to the Church at Rome. The Bible says little about her, but then again – it says a lot about her. Mary is a Roman Christian that Paul greets among many others that were dear to him while he ministered in Rome. She was a woman who bestowed much labour on him and his companions. Take a look at this passage from Romans: 16:3-16:

Romans 16:3–16 Greet Priscilla and Aquila my helpers in Christ Jesus: 4 Who have for my life laid down their own necks: unto whom not only I give thanks, but also all the churches of the Gentiles. 5 Likewise greet the church that is in their house. Salute my wellbeloved Epaenetus, who is the firstfruits of Achaia unto Christ. 6 Greet Mary, who bestowed much labour on us. 7 Salute Andronicus and Junia, my kinsmen, and my fellowprisoners, who are of note among the apostles, who also were in Christ before me. 8 Greet Amplias my beloved in the Lord. 9 Salute Urbane, our helper in Christ, and Stachys my beloved. 10 Salute Apelles approved in Christ. Salute them which are of Aristobulus' household. 11 Salute Herodion my kinsman. Greet them that be of the household of Narcissus, which are in the Lord. 12 Salute Tryphena and Tryphosa, who labour in the Lord. Salute the beloved Persis, which laboured much in the Lord. 13 Salute Rufus chosen in the Lord, and his mother and mine. 14 Salute Asyncritus, Phlegon, Hermas, Patrobas, Hermes, and the brethren which are with them. 15 Salute Philologus, and Julia, Nereus, and his sister, and Olympas, and all the saints which are with them. 16 Salute one another with an holy kiss. The churches of Christ salute you.

Do you see her there, hidden in verse six? This Mary of Rome must have been very active among the believers. I believe she was well known but not often seen. Even so, Paul mentioned her as someone who was an important part of this large group.

WE CAN ONLY IMAGINE

I wonder why there is so little mention of this servant-hearted lady. She must have greatly assisted Paul and the others – notice he said "who bestowed much labour on us." I imagine she was a lady that just did what needed to be done. I imagine she did it without complaining. I imagine she was appreciated by one and all, though perhaps for most of her life she was unnoticed. I imagine she was up before the sun and worked by candlelight when the sun set. I imagine she was kind and gentle and generous. I imagine she was one of those "invisible servants" that we still have in the Church today.

We don't know what this Mary looked like. We are not told of her family. We do not know whether or not she had a husband, or children, or grandchildren, or brothers and sisters. But what we do know is that she was honorable. It was not her "career" that prompted Paul to mention her. He mentioned her because of her character. It was not her wealth or physical appearance that reminded Paul to mention her in that one little verse. She was worthy of praise because of her kindness and Christian work ethic.

We should understand that this special lady was there to serve when she was needed. She did not do it for herself. She is an example of Christ-like servant-hood. She may have been the one who arrived early to stoke the fire and make the meeting place warm, or open the shutters to let the outside air in. She could have been the one who prepared meals for those who were hungry. She might have been the one that went to fetch water from the well – perhaps several times a day. It is possible that she was the one who woke when the cock crowed and made sure the animals were fed. Maybe she got up early and started to make the bread. Then, throughout the day she returned to that task, which probably took four to five hours in Biblical times because they did not have a bakery or grocery store that sold convenience foods. Maybe she had to go out to the yard to harvest the vegetables that were needed to prepare the meals.

THIS MARY IS THE SILENT SERVANT EVEN TODAY

Today she could still be that one that arrives early enough to turn up the heat or power up the air conditioning. She could be the one that polishes the pews or scrubs the floors in the kitchen or the restrooms. Maybe she cleans the toilets regularly or just simply makes sure that there is toilet tissue available for anyone who needs. Maybe she put the coffee on for your Sunday school gathering or even baked those yummy goodies that you enjoy. She could be the lady that is arranging for others to care for your children when you go to worship without distraction. What about the beautiful flowers in the church? Who took care of that? How about the weekly program or bulletin that you look forward to reviewing; someone had to type those up and make copies, right?

You see even in today's Church, we have a need for Mary the Labourer. She is that silent servant. She does not need and usually does not even desire recognition. She is meek, helpful and loyal. You can always count on her to "bestow much labour" without grumbling. How wonderful it is that Paul mentioned her!

THIS MARY IS THE SILENT SERVANT EVEN TODAY

I truly believe this lady was up before the sun so that she could provide all the things behind the scenes for those that she loved. I realize I expounded greatly on this simple verse, but she was a true servant and a woman who most likely did more work than could be mentioned. That is why I call her Mary the Labourer. The following Bible verses are some that describe "Mary the Labourer":

Mark 10:43–45 But so shall it not be among you: but whosoever will be great among you, shall be your minister: 44 And whosoever of you will be the chiefest, shall be servant of all. 45 For even the Son of man came not to be ministered unto, but to minister, and to give his life a ransom for many.

1 Corinthians 13:1 Though I speak with the tongues of men and of angels, and have not charity, I am become as sounding brass, or a tinkling cymbal.

1 Corinthians 15:58 Therefore, my beloved brethren, be ye stedfast, unmoveable, always abounding in the work of the Lord, forasmuch as ye know that your labour is not in vain in the Lord.

Ephesians 6:6–8 Not with eyeservice, as menpleasers; but as the servants of Christ, doing the will of God from the heart; 7 With good will doing service, as to the Lord, and not to men: 8 Knowing that whatsoever good thing any man doeth, the same shall he receive of the Lord, whether he be bond or free.

THINGS TO THINK ABOUT AND DO

1. When I was a child we all knew our neighbors and we visited them regularly. Think about the people in your neighborhood. Do you know them? How can you reach out to them? Can you bake some cookies and deliver them to their door? Can they use a helping hand with something around the house?

23

2. Show some love for the public servants in your community. Have you met the police officers or fire fighters in your district? Do you know what a difficult job they have? How about arranging for some young folks to visit the precinct or fire house with all the fixings for a great meal. I am pretty sure these men and women in community service would not turn that down.

Chapter 6 Mary of Nazareth

By far the most popular Mary in the Bible is Mary of Nazareth. Most people know her as the young virgin girl, whom was born to Jewish parents, that was chosen by God to be the mother of Jesus. While some call her the Mother of Jesus; others call her the Blessed Virgin. Much of the history recorded in the Bible is accepted by most people. Even the account of the angel visiting Mary to announce the conception of Jesus by the Holy Spirit is well known.

TRADITION - THE VIRGIN MARY

In the Catholic Church, members are taught that Mary of Nazareth was a virgin before, during and after the birth of Jesus. In other words, she was a "perpetual virgin" (9). They teach that she and her husband Joseph had no children other than Jesus. This teaching is supported by a document entitled *The Protevangelium of James* (also known as the Infancy Gospels of James and Thomas, contained in the Apocrypha) which was written around A. D. 120 (10). This document is not part of the Holy Bible, yet the entire doctrine of Mary is based upon it.

The Catholic Church also notes that Biblical references to "brethren" or "brothers" of Jesus may be explained by the possibility that Joseph (Mary's husband) was an older man and before he and Mary were wed he had previous children. This was the teaching until the 4th century when a Bible translator by the name of Jerome (11) suggested that these "brethren" might even be cousins of Jesus because it was customary for Jewish families to call cousins "brethren". Regardless of which position you take, when you are a member of the Catholic Church you may choose to believe either of these possibilities about those that the Bible calls Jesus' brethren. This is because the church believes that both views are "compatible with the reality of Mary's perpetual virginity" (8).

A LITTLE FAMILY HISTORY

As we look to the Bible for information regarding Mary of Nazareth we see that not much is known of her personal history, however we can see from the Scriptures that she was from the tribe of Judah of the line of David. Luke lists this genealogy of Jesus through Mary down to David in Luke 3. In contrast, Jesus' ancestry is shown through Joseph in Matthew 1. Take a look:

Matthew 1:16 And Jacob begat Joseph the husband of Mary, of whom was born Jesus, who is called Christ.

Luke 3:23 And Jesus himself began to be about thirty years of age, being (as was supposed) the son of Joseph, which was the son of Heli,

How can this be that Joseph is listed as the son of Jacob in Matthew and the son of Heli in Luke? Two reasons. First, Joseph is listed as the son of Jacob in Matthew because this lineage is Joseph's lineage descending down from Solomon, the son of David (Matthew 6:6). The Gospel of Matthew was written to describe the heirs of the throne from King David to a Jewish audience.

Second, Joseph is listed as the son of Heli in Luke because this lineage is Mary's lineage descending down from Nathan, which was also the son of David (Luke 3:31). The Gospel of Luke was written to describe the lineage of Jesus to a Greek audience.

It is important to understand that being from the tribe of Judah in the line of David is of great significance in order to fulfill the prophecies of a King who would be the Messiah (Genesis 49:10; Psalm 132:11, 2 Samuel 7:12; Matthew 1:1-3; Luke 1:32). So, one of Jesus' credentials as the Messiah is that He had to be verified as a son of King David. Likewise, the biological sons descending from King David would also carry the right to become king. Therefore, the lineage of being a king would have come from Joseph's line through King David. But, there was a problem with the continuation of this lineage with one of Joseph's ancestors.

The Bible records in Joseph's lineage that there was a man by the name of Coniah (Jeconiah in Jeremiah 24:1 and Jeremiah 27:20) who was in the line of Solomon (King David's son). Coniah was cursed because of his wickedness and the Bible says that God declared, "…no man of his seed shall prosper, sitting upon the throne of David…" (See Jeremiah 22:24-30). Therefore, the line of kingship from David through Solomon to Joseph was severed with Coniah. At this moment royalty transferred from the line of Solomon to the line of Nathan, Solomon's brother.

This means that Jesus' biological inheritance of royalty was not received from Joseph, rather it was received from His mother Mary, whom was a descendant of Nathan (Luke 3:31). We see this transfer of biological royalty in both Matthew 1:12 and Luke 3:27 where Salathiel received the inheritance from Solomon's line upon the cursing of Jeconiah (Coniah). From this point forward, the inheritance descended down to Mary, the mother of Jesus.

So then, Jesus is a descendant of David through His mother Mary, making Him the human heir to David's throne. Therefore, Jesus meets the qualification to be given "the throne of his father David" (Luke 1:31-33). Likewise, Jesus, as a Spiritual man, is the Son of our Heavenly Father, conceived by the Holy Spirit and sits on the throne with God the Father (Luke 1:34-35; Hebrews 1:1-8; Revelation 21:5-6; Revelation 22:1-3). Jesus is uniquely qualified to do this because He is fully God and fully man making Him the King of kings (Isaiah 9:6; Luke 1:46-47; John 1:1-14; Philippians 2:5-8; 1 Timothy 6:15; 1 John 5:7 [KJV text]; Revelation 17:14; Revelation 19:16).

THE SPECIAL ANNOUNCEMENT

Before she became the wife of Joseph, Mary resided at Nazareth with her parents. It was there that the angel Gabriel announced to her that she was to be the mother of the "Son of God" as recorded in Luke 1:26-38:

Luke 1:26-38 And in the sixth month the angel Gabriel was sent from God unto a city of Galilee, named Nazareth, 27 To a virgin espoused to a man whose name was Joseph, of the house of David; and the virgin's name was Mary. 28 And the angel came in unto her, and said, Hail, thou that art highly favoured, the Lord is with thee: blessed art thou among women. 29 And when she saw him, she was troubled at his saying, and cast in her mind what manner of salutation this should be. 30 And the angel said unto her, Fear not, Mary: for thou hast found favour with God. 31 And, behold, thou shalt conceive in thy womb, and bring forth a son, and shalt call his name JESUS. 32 He shall be great, and shall be called the Son of the Highest: and the Lord God shall give unto him the throne of his father David: 33 And he shall reign over the house of Jacob for ever; and of his kingdom there shall be no end. 34 Then said Mary unto the angel, How shall this be, seeing I know not a man? 35 And the angel answered and said unto her, The Holy Ghost shall come upon thee, and the power of the Highest shall overshadow thee: therefore also that holy thing which shall be born of thee shall be called the Son of God. 36 And, behold, thy cousin Elisabeth, she hath also conceived a son in her old age: and this is the sixth month with her, who was called barren. 37 For with God nothing shall be impossible. 38 And Mary said, Behold the handmaid of the Lord; be it unto me according to thy word. And the angel departed from her.

After her encounter with Gabriel, Mary departed for a three month visit with her cousin Elisabeth and her husband Zacharias, a priest in the temple in Jerusalem. The journey was about 100 miles from Nazareth to Jerusalem. When Mary entered their house, Elisabeth addressed her as the mother of her Lord (Luke 1:42-45). Mary responded by giving thanks to the Lord:

Luke 1:46-55 And Mary said, My soul doth magnify the Lord, 47 And my spirit hath rejoiced in God my Saviour. 48 For he hath regarded the low estate of his handmaiden: for, behold, from henceforth all generations shall call me blessed. 49 For he that is mighty hath done to me great things; and holy is his name. 50 And his mercy is on them that fear him from generation to generation. 51 He hath shewed strength with his arm; he hath scattered the proud in the imagination of their hearts. 52 He hath put down the mighty from their seats, and exalted them of low degree. 53 He hath filled the hungry with good things; and the rich he hath sent empty away. 54 He hath helped his servant Israel, in remembrance of his mercy; 55 As he spake to our fathers, to Abraham, and to his seed for ever.

In Matthew 1:18-25 we also read the wonderful story of how Joseph was convinced by "the angel of the Lord" (probably Gabriel) in a dream to take Mary as his wife. It was in this dream that he learned that Mary's child was conceived by the Holy Ghost and that the child's name would be called JESUS (Matthew 1:20-21). Soon after this, the decree of Augustus (Luke 2:1-5) required that they should go to Bethlehem of Judah to pay taxes.

Bethlehem was some 80 or 90 miles from Nazareth. When Joseph and Mary arrived they found that all of the guest rooms in the city were occupied by others whom had also come to pay their taxes. Therefore, Mary had to retire to a place among the cattle, where she delivered her son, Whom was called Jesus (Luke 2:6-7; Matthew 1:21). This journey also was a fulfillment of a prophecy about Bethlehem written in Micah 5:2.

MORE ABOUT MARY'S FAMILY

Using the Bible as our book of reference, we can see that Mary of Nazareth, the mother of Jesus, had other children in addition to Jesus. Did you see what the Bible says back in Matthew 1:25? Jesus was her "firstborn son" (Matthew 1:25 "And knew her not till she had brought forth her firstborn son: and he called his name JESUS"). Likewise, I don't think I am reading anything into this simple verse when I conclude that "knew her not till she had brought forth her firstborn son" means that he "knew her" after that. This is because the sentence infers that something else was done after Mary delivered Jesus. In the Biblical sense, "knowing" someone means that a man and a woman have participated in marital relations. When this happens to a virgin, they are no longer a virgin.

So then regarding the other children of Mary, we see in the Bible that even people from Jesus' home town knew that he had brothers and sisters:

Matthew 13:55-56 Is not this the carpenter's son? is not his mother called Mary? and his brethren, James, and Joses, and

Simon, and Judas? 56 And his sisters, are they not all with us? Whence then hath this man all these things?

Mark 6:3 Is not this the carpenter, the son of Mary, the brother of James, and Joses, and of Juda, and Simon? and are not his sisters here with us? And they were offended at him.

THE LATER YEARS

We see little about Mary of Nazareth once Jesus (as an adult) began His public ministry. According to the Bible, she was present at the marriage in Cana. We see her later at Capernaum when she requested to see Jesus while He was speaking to a group of people *(Matthew 12:46-49). This is when Jesus uttered the memorable words, "Who is my mother? and who are my brethren? And he stretched forth his hand toward his disciples, and said, Behold my mother and my brethren!"* We will discuss this in more detail later.

The next time we find Mary of Nazareth is at the cross along with Mary the wife of Cleophas and Mary Magdalene (John 19:25). We see that, while on the cross, Jesus gave the care of his mother over to his disciple John and from that hour John took her into his own house (John 19:26-27). We also see Mary of Nazareth mentioned after Jesus ascended to Heaven. The disciples had just returned from Mount Olivet to an upper room in Jerusalem, as they had been commanded by Jesus (Acts 1:4-13). Mary was part of a little group that joined with the disciples in the upper room to pray (Acts 1:14).

We do not see Mary of Nazareth mentioned anymore in the Bible after these events. We don't know exactly when Mary died and we don't know the circumstances surrounding her death. However, in the absence of this fact, the Catholic Church created what is called the Feast of the Assumption (departure of Mary from this life and taking up of her body into Heaven). This is the principal feast of the Blessed Virgin that is observed by Catholics, although they agree that nothing certain is known of the day, year and manner of her death (6).

THE FAMILY OF GOD

Earlier I mentioned Matthew 12:46-49. Let's look a little closer at that passage and include verse 50. Jesus spoke not of his immediate blood family, but of another family. Take a look:

> Matthew 12:46–50 While he yet talked to the people, behold, his mother and his brethren stood without, desiring to speak with him. 47 Then one said unto him, Behold, thy mother and thy brethren stand without, desiring to speak with thee. 48 But he answered and said unto him that told him, Who is my mother? and who are my brethren? 49 And he stretched forth his hand toward his disciples, and said, Behold my mother and my brethren! 50 For whosoever shall do the will of my Father which is in heaven, the same is my brother, and sister, and mother.

In this passage Jesus redefined the family as being more than just biological. It was a Spiritual family, the brothers and sisters that had been called out of this world by His Heavenly Father. Essentially, He introduced the concept of adoption for those that believe in His redemptive work on the cross. They are adopted into His family as Jesus' brothers and sisters. For believers there is only one family and that is the family of God:

> Romans 8:15–17 For ye have not received the spirit of bondage again to fear; but ye have received the Spirit of adoption, whereby we cry, Abba, Father. 16 The Spirit itself beareth witness with our spirit, that we are the children of God: 17 And if children, then

heirs; heirs of God, and joint-heirs with Christ; if so be that we suffer with him, that we may be also glorified together.

Galatians 3:26 For ye are all the children of God by faith in Christ Jesus.

A PICTURE OF MARY

As we conclude our look at Mary of Nazareth, we see that we do not know much about Mary's physical appearance, but some historical references give us an idea of her character. Mary of Nazareth seems on the surface to be an ordinary Jewish woman whose life was very much like other young Jewish girls. She cooked, sewed and cleaned. She prayed, conversed and served the needs of her family. Yet what we see in the Biblical accounts of Jesus' birth is that Mary's life and character were extraordinary.

Mary of Nazareth was truly a special lady, and God knew! That's why He used her as a vessel to bring Jesus into this world as a man. In addition, He trusted her as a Godly woman, to be a positive influence during the entire thirty-three earthly years of her Son's life. She was there in the beginning and remained with Him, even until His death on the cross.

Mary of Nazareth's extra-ordinariness was not because of anything she did; it was a divine gift. When the angel of the Lord announced to Mary that she would conceive and bring forth a son, she responded as any Godly young woman should. Take a look at how she handled this great honor:

Even though she was not married, Mary was submissive to God the Father in acceptance of the pregnancy:

Luke 1:38 And Mary said, Behold the handmaid of the Lord; be it unto me according to thy word. And the angel departed from her.

Mary was submissive to Jesus the Son as seen in the account of the wedding at Cana:

John 2:3–5 And when they wanted wine, the mother of Jesus saith unto him, They have no wine. 4 Jesus saith unto her, Woman, what have I to do with thee? mine hour is not yet come. 5 His mother saith unto the servants, Whatsoever he saith unto you, do it.

Mary was happy in the Lord:

Luke 1:46–47 And Mary said, My soul doth magnify the Lord, 47 And my spirit hath rejoiced in God my Saviour.

Mary was humble:

Luke 1:48-49 For he hath regarded the low estate of his handmaiden: for, behold, from henceforth all generations shall call me blessed. 49 For he that is mighty hath done to me great things; and holy is his name.

Mary was obedient to the law of God, for by Jewish law, Mary was required to present a sin offering after the birth of a boy child:

Luke 2:22–24 And when the days of her purification according to the law of Moses were accomplished, they brought him to Jerusalem, to present him to the Lord; 23 (As it is written in the law of the Lord, Every male that openeth the womb shall be called holy to the Lord;) 24 And to offer a sacrifice according to that which is said in the law of the Lord, A pair of turtledoves, or two young pigeons.

Leviticus 12:1–8 And the LORD spake unto Moses, saying, 2 Speak unto the children of Israel, saying, If a woman have conceived seed, and born a man child: then she shall be unclean seven days; according to the days of the separation for her infirmity shall she be unclean. 3 And in the eighth day the flesh of his foreskin shall be circumcised. 4 And she shall then continue in the blood of her purifying three and thirty days; she shall touch no hallowed thing, nor come into the sanctuary, until the days of her purifying be fulfilled. 5 But if she bear a maid child, then she shall be unclean two weeks, as in her separation: and she shall continue in the blood of her purifying threescore and six days. 6 And when the days of her purifying are fulfilled, for a son, or for a daughter, she shall bring a lamb of the first year for a burnt offering, and a young pigeon, or a turtledove, for a sin offering, unto the door of the tabernacle of the congregation, unto the priest: 7 Who shall offer it before the LORD, and make an atonement for her; and she shall be cleansed from the issue of her blood. This is the law for her that hath born a male or a female. 8 And if she be not able to bring a lamb, then she shall bring two turtles, or two young pigeons; the one for the burnt offering, and the other for a sin offering: and the priest shall make an atonement for her, and she shall be clean.

Mary's heart would be judged, just as our hearts are judged – she was an ordinary sinner, just like us:

> Luke 2:34–35 And Simeon blessed them, and said unto Mary his mother, Behold, this child is set for the fall and rising again of many in Israel; and for a sign which shall be spoken against; 35 (Yea, a sword shall pierce through thy own soul also,) that the thoughts of many hearts may be revealed.

> Hebrews 4:12–13 For the word of God is quick, and powerful, and sharper than any twoedged sword, piercing even to the dividing asunder of soul and spirit, and of the joints and marrow, and is a discerner of the thoughts and intents of the heart. 13 Neither is there any creature that is not manifest in his sight: but all things are naked and opened unto the eyes of him with whom we have to do.

> Romans 3:23 For all have sinned, and come short of the glory of God;

Mary recognized she needed a Saviour:

> Luke 1:47 And my spirit hath rejoiced in God my Saviour.

God used Mary (an ordinary sinner) to bring forth a son, Jesus, so that through Him we might all be saved from certain death through His death and resurrection (Romans 5:1-9). In essence, God used Mary to bring forth her own Saviour, which is Christ, the Lord (Isaiah 9:6). What a miracle!

We can never give to Jesus physically what Mary gave to Him. She cooperated in God's plan of salvation in a unique way. However, we can welcome Jesus into our lives, our world, our businesses, our homes, and our schools. Essentially, we are still able to "… present your [our] bodies a living sacrifice, holy, acceptable unto God, which is your [our] reasonable service" (Romans 12:1). It is the least that we can do; after all, Jesus chose the nails for us!

CHARACTER TRAIT FOR MARY OF NAZARETH - SUBMISSIVE/OBEDIENT

Of all the Marys in the Bible, I see Mary of Nazareth as the greatest example of submissiveness and obedience. She was obedient to God the Father when she believed Him and prepared herself to deliver the promised Deliverer. She was submissive as she voluntarily put herself under the leadership of Joseph to help raise the Son of God. Here are some Bible verses about submissiveness and obedience that come to mind:

Romans 6:16 Know ye not, that to whom ye yield yourselves servants to obey, his servants ye are to whom ye obey; whether of sin unto death, or of obedience unto righteousness?

Ephesians 5:19–21 Speaking to yourselves in psalms and hymns and spiritual songs, singing and making melody in your heart to the Lord; 20 Giving thanks always for all things unto God and the Father in the name of our Lord Jesus Christ; 21 Submitting yourselves one to another in the fear of God.

Ephesians 6:1 Children, obey your parents in the Lord: for this is right.

Colossians 3:18 Wives, submit yourselves unto your own husbands, as it is fit in the Lord.

2 Corinthians 2:9 For to this end also did I write, that I might know the proof of you, whether ye be obedient in all things.

James 1:22 But be ye doers of the word, and not hearers only, deceiving your own selves.

James 4:7 Submit yourselves therefore to God. Resist the devil, and he will flee from you.

THINGS TO THINK ABOUT AND DO
1. Do you know Jesus as your personal Saviour? If you do, have you thanked Him today for giving His life for yours?

2. Make a special effort within the next couple of days to tell someone who Jesus is and how He can be their Saviour too.

CHAPTER 7 All in All

I am so happy you decided to take the journey through the Bible to discover how easy it is to clear up misunderstandings about Mary. It just takes a little bit of study to get the whole picture, *"For precept must be upon precept, precept upon precept; line upon line, line upon line; here a little and there a little"* (Isaiah 28:10). I have enjoyed looking at these lovely ladies in the Bible; all of them namesakes. Just like me, I hope you were blessed when we studied each one and distinguished the differences and the similarities. Now that we have clarity, we can see the whole picture and what it reveals about each Mary in the Bible.

Be An Example of a Changed Life

Mary Magdalene, committed her life to Jesus after He delivered her from the demons that ruled her life. This is the Mary that has been misunderstood to be a prostitute because of something that was said from the pulpit many years ago. She was not a prostitute; she was just another ordinary woman who was rescued from demons. She was so excited to see Jesus risen from the dead that she could not wait to tell it to everyone she saw. We can learn from her the importance of spreading the news that Jesus is the Deliverer and when we believe in what He did on the cross, we too can be delivered from certain death.

Much like Mary, I was an adult before I was introduced to the most important person in my life. Growing up I heard a lot about Him, but I never knew why He had to die on the cross. I did not know that it was such a personal thing. Since I met my Saviour, I have come to learn that He is the One who sustains me through all of life's ups and downs. Because of Him I am promised eternal life with Him and God our

Father (John 3:36). His name is Jesus and He is the Messiah; the Saviour of the world. He can be your Saviour too.

You see, Jesus is God's Son and on Christmas, we celebrate His birth. The Bible says that no one is good enough to be with God in Heaven when they die because God is holy and His home in Heaven is holy (Romans 3:23). But there is good news, the Bible also says that God is merciful and gracious and He gave His Son to be offered as the Perfect Lamb sacrifice to pay the penalty of death that we all owe because of sin (Romans 6:23). And here's the thing: Jesus did not have to die because He was and is perfect! He did it in our place, as our substitute. Here are some Bible verses that talk about the simple gospel that "Christ died for our sins and rose from the dead":

> 1 Corinthians 15:1-4 Moreover, brethren, I declare unto you the gospel which I preached unto you, which also ye have received, and wherein ye stand; 2 By which also ye are saved, if ye keep in memory what I preached unto you, unless ye have believed in vain. 3 For I delivered unto you first of all that which I also received, how that Christ died for our sins according to the scriptures; 4 And that he was buried, and that he rose again the third day according to the scriptures:

We have a sin debt we cannot pay and Jesus took our debt upon Himself and paid the debt He did not owe. Isn't that good news?

If you believe that Jesus died on the cross to pay for your sins and understand that there is nothing you can do to earn eternal life, then you have the confidence of knowing that when you die you will spend eternity with God and no one can ever take that away from you (Ephesians 1:12-14; 4:30; John 10:27-29; 1 John 5:13). What is stopping you then from believing in the gospel, or good news, of the Bible?

No matter what you have been taught, how bad you are or have been in the past, or what church you attend, salvation is available to everyone, including you! The Bible says, *"For there is no difference between the Jew and the Greek: for the same Lord over all is rich unto all that call upon him. 13 For whosoever shall call upon the name of the Lord shall be saved."* (Romans 10:12-13) Time is short, believe the truth of the gospel today and you can know that you have eternal life *"(For he saith, I have heard thee in a time accepted, and in the day of salvation have I succoured thee: behold, now is the accepted time; behold, now is the day of salvation)"*. (2 Corinthians 6:2; 1 John 5:13).

I'm telling people about Jesus, because His truth is the most important thing that I have ever heard. Just like Mary Magdalene, He changed my life. He can change your life too.

Do Your Part in the Crowd

The Other Mary, although there is little mention of her in the Bible, was honored by being selected as one of three women to first witness our resurrected Jesus. Although she served with other women she realized that she had her own personal part in serving the Lord. Jesus was the object of her loyalty as she stayed at the foot of the cross and then again at the tomb. Because she was part of a trio of Marys it is easy to understand how her part could have been confused with someone else. In fact, this may be why this Mary is frequently misunderstood and often confused with Mary of Nazareth.

From this Other Mary we can learn the importance of having a personal relationship with Jesus as the priority in our life. However, relationships must be cultivated and to have a friend we must spend time with them. We can be a friend of God by spending time daily in the Word with Him. This is where we learn what He wants us to know about Him and serves as the foundation for everything we do as a believer. This is why He called holy men to write down His words in the Bible as they were moved by the Holy Spirit (2 Peter 1:16-21) so that His words will move us to do our part in the crowd.

Take Time to Love

Mary of Bethany is the one who washed the feet of Jesus. She poured precious oil on His body to prepare for His coming burial. She was chastised by onlookers for her devotion to her Master. She and her brother and sister were honored to have Jesus as a close personal friend. Her act of humility and love was so touching and important that Jesus said she would be remembered for what she had done. It is this Mary that is so easily misunderstood and confused as Mary Magdalene because so many believed the words of a man instead of studying for themselves from the Word of God. This is the Mary that I was looking for to discuss in my devotional at the Ladies' Tea that I mentioned in the beginning of this book. At the Tea, I began with a song which was popular at the time, the lyrics of the song spoke of how important it is for us to love the Lord completely, just like when we completely empty the contents of an alabaster box. We can learn from Mary of Bethany that sometimes we just need to take time to "love" and not be worried about all that other stuff.

Practice Generosity and Hospitality

The generous Mary the Mother of John Mark had the means and wherewithal to offer her home as a meeting place for the family of God. Her motives might be misunderstood by those outside of the Church, but we that are inside can see that her gift of hospitality can teach us that giving sometimes means opening your house to a fellow brother or sister. Those that are doing the full-time work of the ministry often travel to meetings and need a place to stay. You should consider if opening your home is something that would be a blessing to others.

Be The Silent Servant

Mary the Labourer is mentioned only in one small little verse in the Bible, but her heart is anything but small. She is the Silent Servant – the one that is "backstage" and takes care of all those little things that we take for granted when we go to spend time at our local church or any church sponsored event. She is the "chief cook and bottle washer" of sorts and does not desire recognition. The misunderstanding in this Mary lies in the fact that things don't just happen by magic. A Church is a body with many members; each member must have a part in how that Church functions. Without Mary the Labourer you might be cold during the message on Sunday because somebody forgot to turn up the heat. Without Mary the Labourer you might wonder what's happening in the Church because nobody prepared the bulletin or program for your reading. Without Mary the Labourer the table won't be ready for the "carry in" dinner because there was not anybody to do it. I read this little poem once that reminds me of this Mary:

> There was an important job to be done and *Everybody* was sure that *Somebody* would do it. *Anybody* could have done it, but *Nobody* did it. *Somebody* got angry with that because it is *Everybody's* job. *Everybody* thought *Anybody* could do it. But *Nobody* realized that *Everybody* wouldn't do it. It ended that *Everybody* blamed *Somebody* when *Nobody* did what *Everybody* could have. (Anonymous)

So what can you do? Certainly everybody could do something.

Be Obedient and Submissive to God's Plan

Mary of Nazareth was extraordinary but not of herself. She submitted to God and He used Mary to bring forth her own Saviour! We can never give of our body like Mary did, but we can practice what Paul encouraged the Church at Rome to do, *"present your bodies a living sacrifice, holy, acceptable unto God, which is your reasonable service"* (Romans 12:1). As a young virgin she delivered her Son and then when He was a man, He delivered her – what a miracle! However, she gave completely of herself, but was powerless as she witnessed the brutal murder of her Son as He gave completely of Himself.

Sometimes we think that the things that we do don't make any difference and people may even redefine to others what we really are. Mary was no exception and those who redefine her life in matters of her being a perpetual virgin fail to recognize this. Some of the greatest things that anyone can do on behalf of the Lord do not need embellishment that contradicts the truth of the Bible. Mary was used by God to fulfill the simple truth of Isaiah 7:14, to deliver Immanuel to the world -- not to bring attention to herself. With the exception of the virgin birth, Mary was just an ordinary sinner, blessed among women with the honor to deliver the Deliver.

Final Thoughts

Understanding the truth of the Bible, comparing scriptures one to another is what keeps us from following things that have been made famous by man's words. God's words are available for our learning and teaching. By the power of the Holy Spirit and the written Word of God as I studied, the confusion that I once had about the Marys in the Bible has been cleared up.

I hope that now we can see that something like Mary Misunderstood can easily happen when we are ignorant to the truth of the Bible. I realize that I have touched on some controversial things; however, I was convicted that I must share what I learned. This way others will not fall into the same trap that I almost fell into because I listened to someone else and had not studied it out for myself.

Although we cannot physically walk with Jesus today, we can still learn from Him by reading His words. One who is a learner is called a disciple. Jesus said to the Jews who believed on Him in John 8:31-32 *"…If ye continue in my word, then are ye my disciples indeed; 32 And ye shall know the truth, and the truth shall make you free."* Jesus was speaking before the Bible was even written. During the time when Jesus walked the earth, His disciples lived by the truth that He spoke to them as He taught them in person.

As you walk with the Lord you ought to begin understanding more and more of the Bible. God teaches us what we need to know when we are daily in the Word. Reading and studying is how we grow out of being baby Christians into mature Christians, understanding the doctrines of the Bible.

Isaiah 28:9 Whom shall he teach knowledge? and whom shall he make to understand doctrine? them that are weaned from the milk, and drawn from the breasts.

Pamela Rose Williams

Resources

(1) The Da Vinci Code (film). Retrieved from
https://en.wikipedia.org/wiki/The_Da_Vinci_Code (film)
(2) Homily 33 is recorded in Homilariun in evangelia, Lob. 11, Patrologia
Latina, bol. 76. (Paris: J.P.Migne, 1844-1864), cols. 1238-1246
(3) Williams, Mary Alice. "Mary Magdalene". PBS: Religion and Ethics.
November 21, 2003. Episode no. 712. Web: 22 December 2009
(4) Bible Walks (n.d.). from http://www.biblewalks.com/Sites/magdala.html
(5) Map of Ancient Israel - Magdala - Bible History Online. (n.d.). from
http://www.bible-history.com/geography/ancient-israel/magdala.html
(6) The Feast of the Assumption of the Blessed Virgin Mary, 15 August; also
called in old liturgical books Pausatio, Nativitas (for heaven), Mors,
Depositio, Dormitio S. Mariae.
http://www.newadvent.org/cathen/02006b.htm
(7) Maps of Ancient Israel - Bethany - Bible History Online (n.d.). from
http://www.bible-history.com/geography/ancient-israel/bethany.html
(8) Germano, M. P. (n.d.). Retrieved, from
http://www.bibarch.com/Biographs/Ancient/MaryJMsmom.htm
(9) Tracts. (n.d.). from http://www.catholic.com/tract/mary-ever-virgin
(10) Hock, R. F. (1995). The Infancy Gospels of James and Thomas: With
introduction, notes, and original text featuring the New Scholars Version
translation.
(11) 131 Christians Everyone Should Know by Mark Galli and Ted Olsen
(Holman reference 2000)

46

About the Author

Pamela Rose Williams is a wife, mother and grandmother. She and her husband, Dr. Michael L. Williams, have served in Christian ministry since 2001. She has a Bachelor's Degree in Christian Education and spends most of her time as a professional editor and writer, working with many Christian authors and artists. She also uses her extensive experience in information technology providing Christ-centered teaching tools and resources for people all over the world. Learn more about Pamela Rose at ChristianityEveryDay.com.

Pamela Rose Williams

How did you like this book?

Tell others what you think of the book by taking a few minutes rate the book and share your thoughts on Amazon.com. Thank you.

Christianity Every Day
www.christianityeveryday.com